Backyard
ENCYCLOPEDIA

Rufus Bellamy

Crabtree Publishing Company

www.crabtreebooks.com

Author: Rufus Bellamy
Editor: Crystal Sikkens
Project coordinator: Kathy Middleton
Production coordinator: Ken Wright
Prepress technician: Margaret Amy Salter
Series consultant: Gill Matthews

Picture credits:
Dreamstime: Claudio Baldini 15t, Clearviewstock 8–9,
    Marika Eglite 9t, Noah Golan 14–15b, Irochka 1br, 16br,
    Steve Mann 19, Megejaz 21r, Anette Linnea Rasmussen 13b,
    Jean Schweitzer 2, Kimberly Skeie 1bl, 16bl,
    Ljupco Smokovski 16c, Maxim Tupikov 11b,
    Olga Zinatova 8b
FLPA: Michael Durham / MindenPictures 20t
Istockphoto: (Cover) Mammamaart, Catman73 4l,
    Danny Chung 1–24, Eric Isselee 7t, Hans Slegers 17br,
    Andrew Whittle 6bl, Alexei Zaycev 18t
Shutterstock: (Cover) Tischenko Irina, 2happy 6br,
    Abrakadabra 17bl, Antonio S 5t, Argus 17bc,
    Elena Butinova 18b, Laurent Dambies 20–21,
    Sergiy Goruppa 1b, 16b, Jeff Gynane 14b,
    Hardtmuth 1t, 16t, Petr Jilek 10t, Els Jooren 4r,
    Wendy Kaveney Photography 17t, David Kelly 5b,
    Liew Weng Keong 11t, Letty17 13t, Mashe 12t,
    Amy Myers 6t, PeapPop 15b, Kateryna Potrokhova 8t,
    Sally Scott 14t, Lori Skelton 3r, Studiotouch 20b,
    Szabo Photography 21t, Andy Z 12–13b

Every effort has been made to trace copyright holders and to obtain their permission for use of copyright material. The authors and publishers would be pleased to rectify any error or omission in future editions All the Internet addresses given in this book were correct at the time of going to press. The author and publishers regret any inconvenience caused if addresses have changed or sites have ceased to exist, but can accept no responsibility for any such changes.

Library and Archives Canada Cataloguing in Publication

Bellamy, Rufus
    Backyard encyclopedia / Rufus Bellamy.

(Crabtree connections)
Includes index.
ISBN 978-0-7787-9945-0 (bound).--ISBN 978-0-7787-9967-2 (pbk.)

    1. Garden ecology--Juvenile literature. 2. Garden animals--Juvenile literature. I. Title. II. Series: Crabtree connections.

QH541.5.G37B44 2010   j577.554   C2010-901508-8

Library of Congress Cataloging-in-Publication Data

Bellamy, Rufus.
    Backyard encyclopedia / Rufus Bellamy.
        p. cm. -- (Crabtree connections)
    Includes index.
    ISBN 978-0-7787-9967-2 (pbk. : alk. paper) -- ISBN 978-0-7787-9945-0 (reinforced library binding : alk. paper)
    1. Garden animals--Juvenile literature. I. Title. II. Series: Crabtree connections.

QL119.B45 2011
591.75'54--dc22
                                    2010008051

Crabtree Publishing Company
www.crabtreebooks.com   1-800-387-7650

Printed in the U.S.A. / 062010 / WO20100815

Published in Canada
Crabtree Publishing
616 Welland Ave.
St. Catharines, Ontario
L2M 5V6

Published in the United States
Crabtree Publishing
PMB 59051
350 Fifth Avenue, 59th Floor
New York, New York 10118

Contents

Backyard Safari

Come on a backyard safari to discover the world of wildlife in your backyard, schoolyard, or local park.

Wildlife secrets: In this book you'll get to discover the secrets of amazing animals and plants that live just outside your window.

Seasons: The natural world changes as the **seasons** change, so there is always something new to see.

Important places: Backyards and green spaces in towns and cities are very important. They provide animals with food, water, and a place to live.

Blackbirds visit backyards to look for food.

Squirrels hunt for nuts and seeds in backyards.

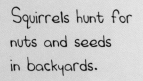

Wildlife havens: Many animals are finding it more difficult to live in the countryside. This means that millions of backyards in North America are now havens for a lot of wild animals such as birds and frogs.

Green gardening:

It is important to make backyards as wildlife-friendly as possible. There is a lot you can do—from putting up a birdhouse, to making sure there are plants that provide food for insects, birds, and other animals.

The io moth is just one of the amazing animals you might see in a backyard.

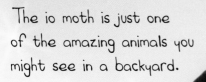

On the Lawn

A lawn may not seem like a good place for wildlife, but look carefully and you'll be surprised at what you can find.

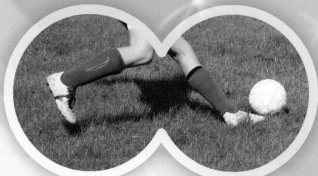

Grass: Like other green plants, grass makes its own food using water, energy from sunlight, and **carbon dioxide** from the air.

Take a look at the grass under your feet the next time you play soccer.

Visitors: Lawns are places where you might catch a glimpse of the larger animals that sometimes visit backyards, such as rabbits and raccoons. Birds also visit lawns to look for insects and worms to eat.

Many birds eat worms they find in lawns.

Lawns: Many lawns are made up of three or four types of grass. Other plants such as moss, clover, and daisies also grow in lawns.

Worms: Under the lawn worms are busy eating the soil. This breaks it up and makes it better for plants to grow.

Small animals: A lot of small animals, such as ants, slugs, and snails, are found on lawns. Some animals are not welcome. For example, grubs feed on grass roots and can damage lawns. Grubs turn into beetles.

Lunch on the lawn

Ants, slugs, and snails are just some of the small animals you can find in the grass. Birds and other animals like lawns because the short grass makes it easier for them to find food.

In the Hedge

The overgrown bushes around the edges of backyards, parks, and playgrounds are great for animals.

Birds: Different shrubs and bushes attract a variety of birds. Birds use hedges to build nests, hide from **predators**, and find food to eat.

Nettles: Nettles can give you a nasty sting, but they are very good for insects. The caterpillars of several butterflies and moths, including the mouse moth, eat nettles.

Butterflies, such as this red admiral, lay eggs that hatch into hungry caterpillars.

Spiders trap food, such as flies and other insects, in their webs.

Berries: Birds, insects, and other animals feed on the berries that grows on bushes. This fruit contains **seeds** that animals often help to spread out. New plants grow from these seeds.

Spiders: Spiders spin webs using "spider silk" that they make in their bodies.

Ivy: The ivy plant is a great climber and can grow up a wall, fence, or tree. Climbing plants like this provide a place for animals to hide.

Spotlight on homes

Animals need places in which they can hide, rest, and make their homes. That is why it is important to leave wild areas for animals in backyards, parks, and playgrounds.

Up a Tree

Trees, such as the mighty oak, are home to many different animals—from the tiniest insects to large animals such as squirrels.

Fruit trees: Apple, pear, cherry, and other fruit trees provide us with things to eat. Many animals, including birds and butterflies, eat fruit, too.

Large trees are a high-rise home for backyard animals.

Evergreen: Trees such as spruces and firs (the kind that are often used as Christmas trees) keep their leaves all year. These are called "evergreens." The trees that lose their leaves in fall are called **deciduous**.

Nests: Birds, such as robins, build their nests in the branches of trees. Other birds, such as the chickadee, nest in holes. Putting up a sheltered ledge or birdhouse is a great way to give birds like this a home.

Old wood: A pile of old wood attracts many insects including termites and beetles. It is also a place where animals such as toads and newts can find shelter.

Carpenter ants like dead, damp wood. They often live in rotting logs.

Fungus: Many types of fungus feed on dead and **decaying** wood.

Thirsty trees

Trees need water to live and grow. They take in water from the soil through their roots. The roots of a tree spread far out into the soil below it.

In the Flower Bed

The flowers and shrubs in a flower bed are important for butterflies and many other insects.

Nectar: Flowers contain sweet **nectar**. Many insects visit flowers to collect nectar, which they use for food.

Ladybugs can eat thousands of aphids in just one year.

Roses: Backyard flowers, such as roses, have been bred for their look and smell. Some gardeners also like to grow wild flowers, such as lilies and poppies.

Flowers and insects: Flowers make a powder called **pollen**. This is often rubbed off on insects such as bees. The bees then carry the pollen from flower to flower as they fly. If this did not happen, many plants could not make seeds.

Daffodils flower
in early spring.

Bulbs: Some flowers, such as daffodils, grow from an underground **bulb**. The plant uses food stored in the bulb to grow.

Ladybugs: Ladybugs are a gardener's friend because they eat aphids and other insects that eat flowers. Many other small animals can be found in a flower bed, including centipedes, beetles, and flies.

Spotlight on snowdrops

The flowers of different backyard plants appear at different times during the year. Snowdrops appear at the end of winter.

In the Vegetable Garden

Vegetable gardens are where gardeners grow things to eat. They are also full of interesting things to discover.

The vegetable garden is a great place to find food—for both animals and people!

Plant parts: We eat a lot of different parts of plants. For example, we eat the roots of carrot plants, the leaves of lettuce, and the stems of celery.

Potato: A potato is actually an underground food store for the potato plant. We dig them up and use them as food.

Compost: A garden compost pile is made up of old leaves, cut grass, and other garden waste. Worms and other small animals turn this waste into rich compost. This is put back into the soil to help plants grow.

Pests: Many animals like to help themselves to food from a vegetable garden. Lettuce is a particular favorite of slugs and snails. Birds will eat newly planted seeds if they get the chance.

Peas: Look inside a pea pod and you will find seeds from which new plants grow.

A compost pile is a great way to recycle backyard waste.

Each pea pod contains several peas.

Spotlight on slugs

Slugs are a pest to gardeners, but an important source of food for birds and other animals, such as skunks. Slugs leave trails of slime behind them, so you can see where they have been.

In the Yard

Even an empty backyard with no grass and few plants can hold surprises for a wildlife explorer.

Night visitors: When it gets dark, a bright outdoor light, or lit window, will attract many insects, including midges and moths. Bats eat these insects.

Moths: Most moths fly at night and rest with their wings folded flat. Most butterflies rest with their wings above their backs—this is one way to tell moths and butterflies apart.

Ants: Ants are common backyard visitors. They are small, but strong—they can carry over ten times their own body weight.

Ants like to hide under stones and in wall cracks.

It is important to feed birds in the winter when food is scarce.

Bird feeder: An easy way to attract birds into any yard is to put up a bird feeder full of food, such as seeds and nuts. Birds also need water, so put out a shallow dish of clean water, too.

Moths use the light of the Moon to help them get around at night.

Dandelions: Dandelions grow in unexpected places—even in the gaps between patio stones.

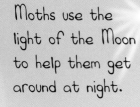

Dangerous cats

Many backyard birds and other animals are killed by cats, which often hunt them for food. Putting a bell around a cat's neck is a good way to warn birds so they stay safe.

By the Pond

Many animals and plants need the water
in a pond to live. It provides them with
somewhere to find food and make a home.

Living in water: Ponds are
full of animals. Some, such as
pond snails, eat plants.
Water striders run across
the surface of the water
to hunt other insects.

Danger: Ponds can be dangerous,
so be careful near them. Ponds can also be
a problem for some animals looking for food,
such as chipmunks. It is important to provide
a way for these animals to climb out.

Water striders
are covered in
hairs, which help
them stay on
top of the
water's surface.

Frogs and toads lay
their eggs in ponds.

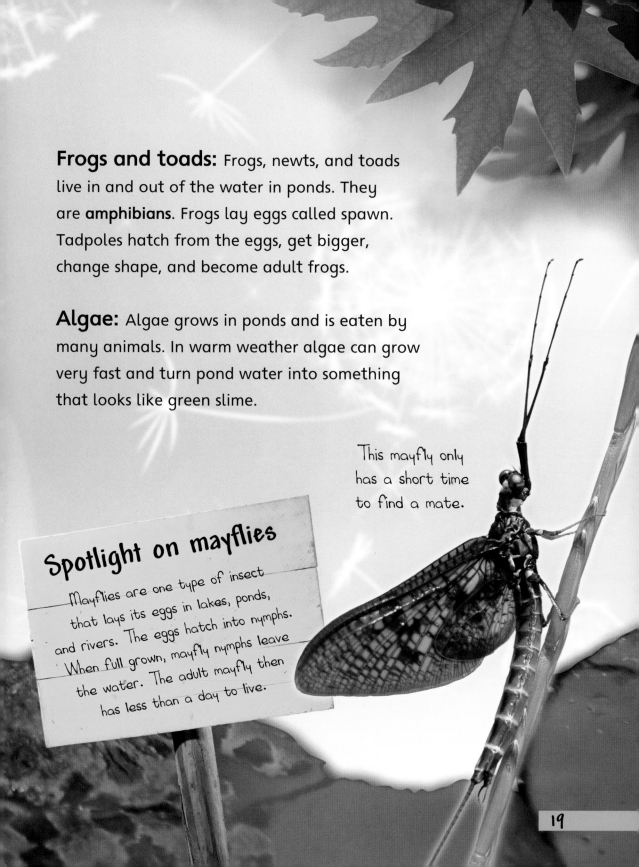

Frogs and toads: Frogs, newts, and toads live in and out of the water in ponds. They are **amphibians**. Frogs lay eggs called spawn. Tadpoles hatch from the eggs, get bigger, change shape, and become adult frogs.

Algae: Algae grows in ponds and is eaten by many animals. In warm weather algae can grow very fast and turn pond water into something that looks like green slime.

This mayfly only has a short time to find a mate.

Spotlight on mayflies

Mayflies are one type of insect that lays its eggs in lakes, ponds, and rivers. The eggs hatch into nymphs. When full grown, mayfly nymphs leave the water. The adult mayfly then has less than a day to live.

In the Air

Backyards and parks are great places to see insects, birds, and other flying creatures.

Bats: Bats make high-pitched sounds that bounce off anything nearby. When bats pick up these echoes they know what is around them. This is how they catch insects in the dark.

Bats are usually seen in backyards at nighttime.

Birds in a backyard:

Birds use backyards to search for food and water, and raise a family. Sparrows, starlings, blackbirds, and blue jays are among the common backyard birds.

Robin: Birds, such as the robin, sing to attract a mate and to mark out a territory. Male robins will fight fiercely to defend their territories.

Using binoculars will help you to spot birds such as this robin.

Migrating birds: Many birds are great travelers. Birds, such as Canada geese, **migrate** thousands of miles to warmer countries in the fall. When winter is over, the birds fly back to their home countries.

Spotting birds: If you want to get to know the birds that visit your backyard, sit quietly in a hidden spot. You'll need a bird book to help you name the birds you see.

Spotlight on dragonflies

Dragonflies and damselflies are some of the most beautiful flying insects. They are also amazing hunters. They eat other insects, such as mosquitoes.

Glossary

amphibians Types of animals that spend part of their time on land and part of their time in the water

bulb Part of a plant that stores food

carbon dioxide Gas that occurs naturally in the air

decaying When a plant or animal has died and is breaking up into smaller and smaller pieces

deciduous Trees or shrubs that lose their leaves for part of the year

migrate When animals move in search of food, a place to breed, or to escape cold weather

nectar Sugar-rich liquid produced by plants to attract insects

pollen A powdery substance produced by flowers

predators Animals that hunt other animals for food

seasons The divisions of the year—spring, summer, fall, and winter are the seasons in North America

seeds Tiny "baby" plants from which a new plant will grow if conditions are right

Further Information

Web sites

Find out more about the birds, animals, and insects in your backyard at:

www.backyardnature.net/

Find out how much you know about your backyard animals with a fun game at:

www.sheppardsoftware.com/content/animals/quizzes/ kidscorner/animal_games_backyard_flower_large.html

Books

Animals in the Garden by Mari Schuh.
Capstone (2010).

Backyard Bugs by Jenny Vaughan.
Tick Tock Books (2009).

Microscopic Life in the Garden by Brian Ward.
Franklin Watts (2007).

Living things in my back yard by Bobbie Kalman.
Crabtree Publishing (2008).

Index